CATS LOVE JEWELRY

by Jeremy Hoang

illustrated by 18/1 graphics studio

Copyright © 2025 by Jeremy Hoang.

All rights reserved.

No part of this publication may be reproduced, distributed, or transmitted in any form or by any means, including photocopying, recording, or other electronic or mechanical methods, without the prior written permission of the publisher, except as permitted by U.S. copyright law. For permission requests, contact [include publisher/author contact info].

The story, all names, characters, and incidents portrayed in this production are fictitious. No identification with actual persons (living or deceased), places, buildings, and products is intended or should be inferred.

Book Cover & illustrations by 18/1 Graphics Studio

1st edition 2025

Dedication

To my wife and our children:
smart, beautiful, and loving.

HEY, KID!

Did you know that cats love jewelry?
They love necklaces and bracelets.
They love big diamonds and small diamonds.

By night, they would sneak into town, their paws silent against the streets, to **"BORROW"** the shiniest of jewels from unsuspecting townsfolk.

Mrs. Whiskers laughed and said, "My darlings, with treasures like these, we could start our very own jewelry store!"

The cats meowed in agreement, their eyes gleaming with dreams of *diamonds and pearls.*

Instead of falling for the **TRAP,** they left a heap of catnip in their wake, much to the townsfolk's confusion.

Embracing their new identity, Mrs. Whiskers transformed her cottage into a bustling
CATNIP SHOP,

where the cats served as the most charming sales **PURR-SONALITIES.**

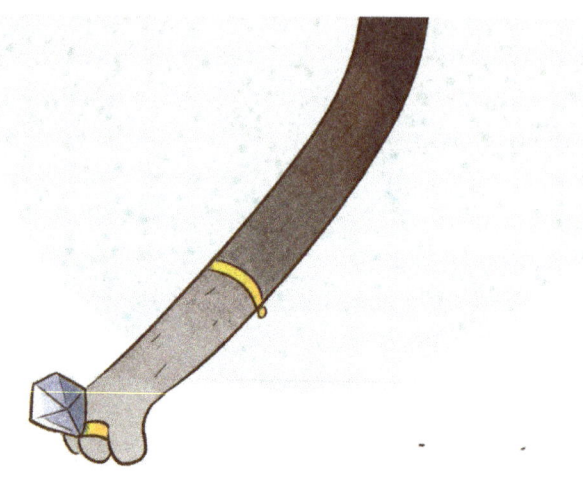

With their newfound wealth, the cats adorned themselves with the jewels they had collected, turning every day into a

DAZZLING CELEBRATION.

Now, with all the jewelry "in their paws," the cats joyfully dressed themselves with sparkling necklaces, gleaming rings, and shimmering bracelets.

Each cat took pride in their *unique style*, flaunting their treasures with a graceful strut.

Their adventures did not end there. The cats decided to host a grand cat **FASHION SHOW,** strutting down a makeshift runway in their sparkly necklaces and fluffy hats.

The townsfolk gathered, curious and amused, as the feline models flaunted their "borrowed" jewelry.

Not content with fashion alone, the cats formed a band known as **"THE PURRFECT HARMONY,"** using pots and pans to create the most delightful meow-sic.

leading the cats on a *merry chase* through the town.

The pursuit was *wild and full of chaos*, but it ended in laughter,

www.ingramcontent.com/pod-product-compliance
Lightning Source LLC
LaVergne TN
LVHW070604070526
838199LV00012B/480